I0111283

海豚出版社
DOLPHIN BOOKS
CICG | 中国国际传播集团

Published in the United States by Flying Tiger Press. Published in China by Dolphin Books.

Original Chinese edition Managed by: Jin Yongbiao and Wu Wei

© 2024 Flying Tiger Press

Flying Tiger Press supports copyright and deeply thanks you for purchasing an authorized edition of this book. Copyright is not just a legal tool but a vital aspect of cultural exchange and preservation. It ensures that creators and custodians of stories, especially those as culturally significant as the King Gesar legend, are recognized and rewarded for their work. This, in turn, enables the sharing and appreciation of diverse cultural heritages globally. Your support of copyright integrity contributes directly to a vibrant, diverse cultural landscape, allowing stories from all corners of the world to be told and preserved for future generations.

Flying Tiger Press is the Trademark of Jiang Boyan LLC.

Flying Tiger Press' books are available at special discounts when purchased in bulk for premiums and sales promotions as well as for educational use. For details, please contact us at info@flyingtigerpress.org.

Library of Congress Cataloging-in-Publication Data has been applied for.

Hardcover ISBN: 978-1-963417-12-8
Paperback ISBN: 978-1-963417-22-7
E-book ISBN: 978-1-963417-02-9

Printed in the United States of America
First Edition

The first graphic novel of King Gesar, adapted from the world's longest epic *Gesar*. A Tibetan equivalent of *Odyssey*, the ancient epic remains a living oral literature and has been inscribed in 2009 (4.COM) on UNESCO's Representative List of the Intangible Cultural Heritage of Humanity.

The 10-volume series *The Legend of King Gesar* tells of Gesar's birth, his early years and love stories, and his fight against malevolent forces. Born to be a hero, Gesar has been sent down to the human world to conquer monsters and liberate the people, but he is framed by his uncle and sent into exile. Can he finish his mission?

Winner of Best Comic Award of the 5th Asian Youth Animation & Comics Contest (AYACC)

Winner of Grand Master Prize at the 2nd Master Cup International Illustration Biennial

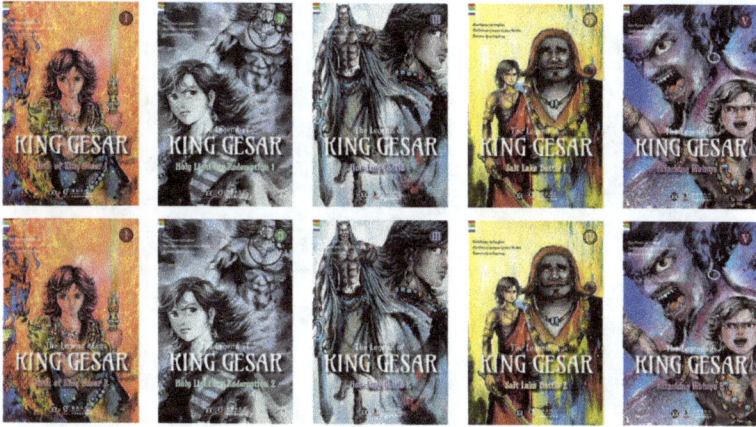

Gyanpian Gyamco is a specialist in researching and translating the Tibetan epic *King Gesar* and Tibetan contemporary literature and a doctoral supervisor at the Institute of Ethnic Literature, Chinese Academy of Social Sciences.

Quan Yingsheng is a contemporary artist and member of China Artists Association. He has been making comics, animations, ink paintings and Zen paintings for more than 20 years. His comics and ink paintings have won many awards. He was involved in making 52 episodes of *Journey to the West* produced by China Central Television (CCTV).

Jin Yongbiao is a book and animation planner. He was a journalist, full-time literary translator, editor of a literary magazine, book editor, deputy editor-in-chief and vice president of a publishing house.

Wu Wei is the former Deputy Director of the Third Bureau of China's State Council Information Office and the former Deputy General Manager of China National Publications Import and Export Corporation. Her works include *Biography of King Gesar*.

An Introduction to the Principal Characters

Ngada Namo:
the younger sister of Nortsam in charge of defending the first pass of the Demon State in the north. After Gesar conquered them, she married him.

Nortsam:
King of the Demon State in the north and one of the four major demon kings.

Chin'en:
Minister of the Right of the Demon State in the north.

Cecho:
a general of the Demon State in the north.

Mofi:
a lad in a village of the Demon State in the north.

Dainma:
a skillful archer and a famous warrior of the State of Ling.

Prince of the White Tent:
Head of the three kings of the State of Hor.

Tsinpa Merotse:
Commander of the State of Hor.

CONTENTS

Chapter 1   Black and White World ------006

Chapter 2   Female Devil ------------------026

Chapter 3   Dream that Has Never Gone - 046

Chapter 4   Death Pasture---------------- 066

Chapter 5   Soul-Housing Tree ---------- 086

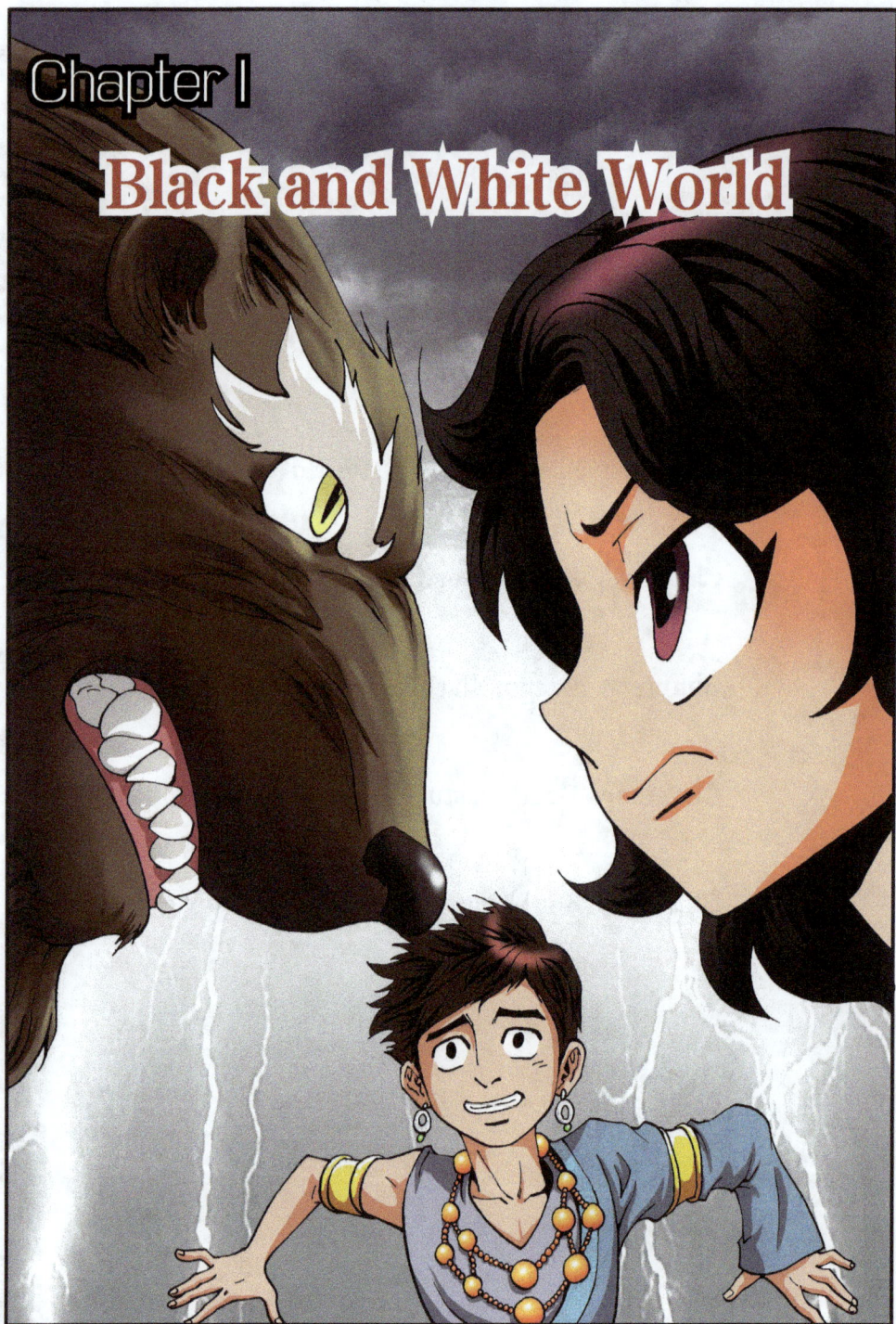

Chapter I
Black and White World

At the beginning...

There was a plain called Cairan Morbo in the Yarkang area, north of the Tibetan land.

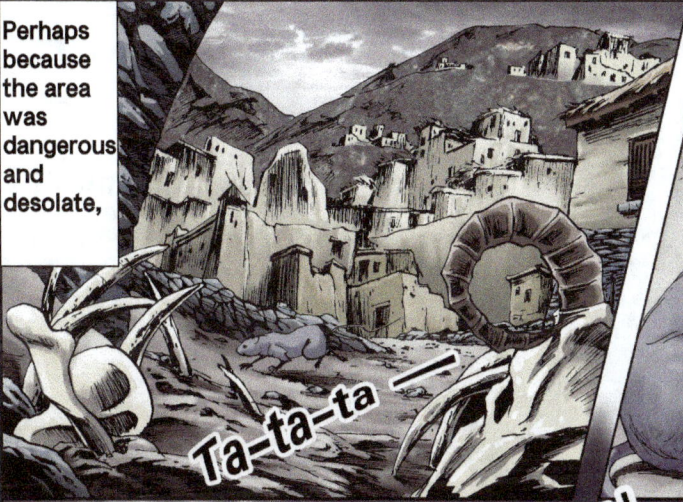

Perhaps because the area was dangerous and desolate,

Ta-ta-ta —

It was also known as...

Ghost Land!

Rumbling!

Whooshing—

Whooshing—

Purring── Sleep?

Purring── Purring

Gyaingar Pebo, you can't die!

Getting rid of hunger by sleeping?

It is a good idea.

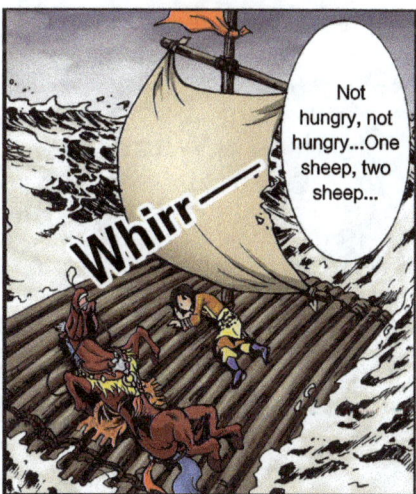

Whirr──

Not hungry, not hungry...One sheep, two sheep...

What?

010

Whooshing!

We come from the State of Ling.

※ Note: Gesar founded the State of Ling after he won the throne in the horse race.

We are starving. Do you have something to eat?

It seems we have escaped.

Well, are you on a trip?

Do go back. It is too dangerous here.

No, I come here to look for a girl.

She is Sengcham Cholmo.

Girl?

All the young women have been captured by the Demon King.

My elder sister has also been...

Help!

Haha! Haha! Capture them all!

Run!

King!

Let me take care of her for you.

King!

Monster, I'll fight you!

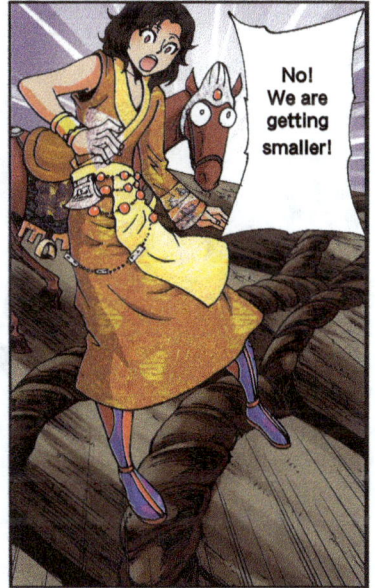

Paw!
Paw!
Paw!

Pa!

Whooshing—

What
is it
called?

Whooshing—

New
move.
I can do
that too!

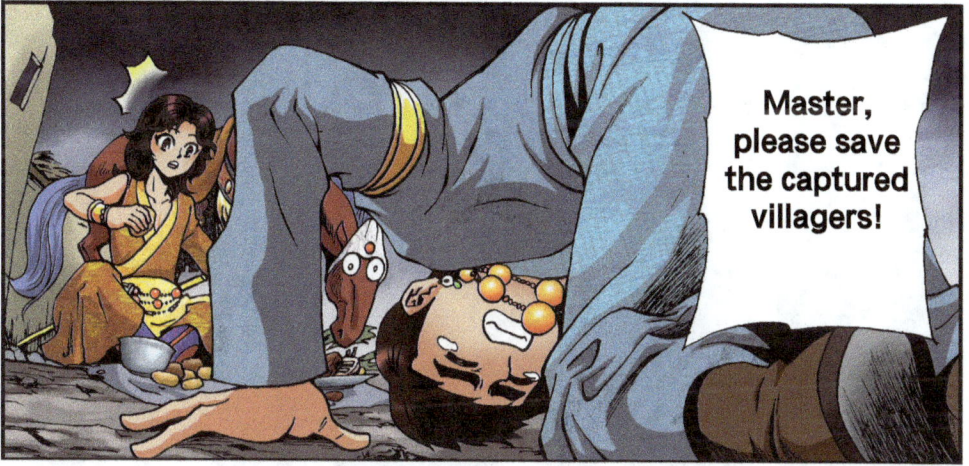

Master, please save the captured villagers!

By the time I return, my elder sister and villagers might have been killed already.

Moreover, I don't know whether I can defeat the demon.

Don't call me master.

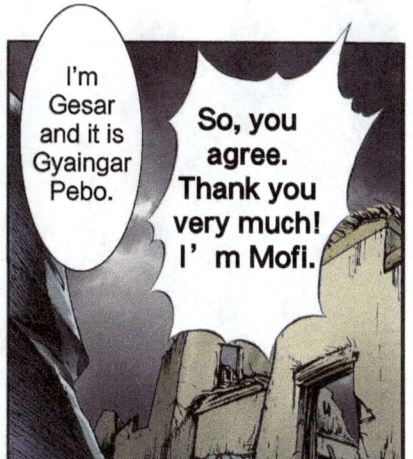

I'm Gesar and it is Gyaingar Pebo.

So, you agree. Thank you very much! I'm Mofi.

I should be...?

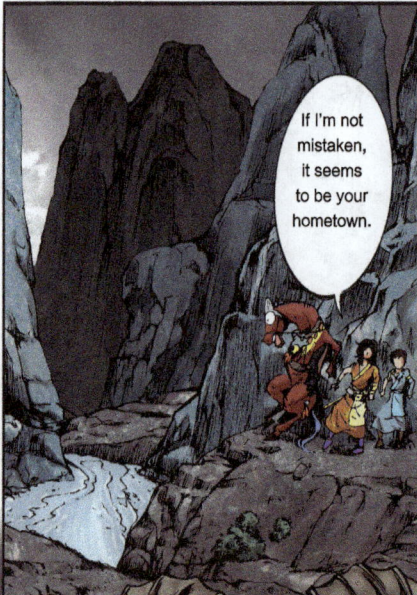

If I'm not mistaken, it seems to be your hometown.

Yes, but...

Are you a local person?

Don't change the subject!

The first pass of the Demon State

It is also the first time that I have ever been here.

Anybody here?

It is so terrible here. Let's make a detour.

I'm not full..

Is that guy human?

Anything to eat?

Chapter 2

Female Devil

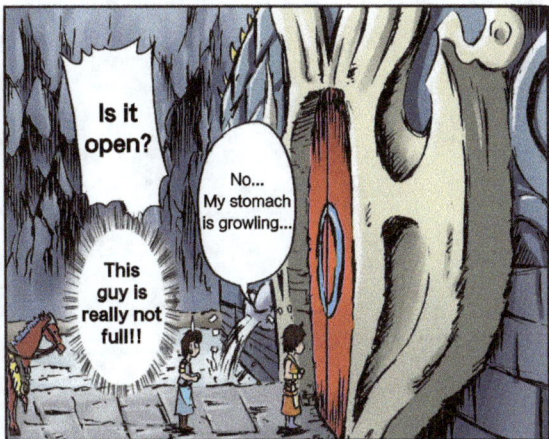

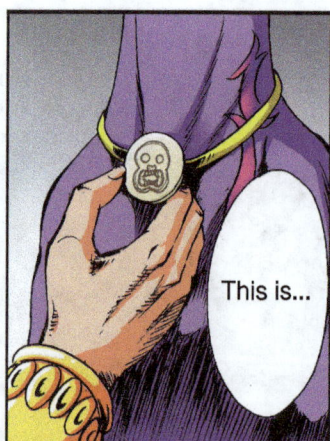

Pa!

Cha!

Doggie! Weren't you very arrogant just now?

Be my supper, OK?

Who is there?

Ngada Namo

How dare you be so rude to my dog!

Because you have to die whether you refuse to fight or whether you are defeated!

If you win, you will be my husband!

What?

Er, how can I do that?

You agree!

Swish!

Brat! How dare you belittle me?

You scared? Make your move!

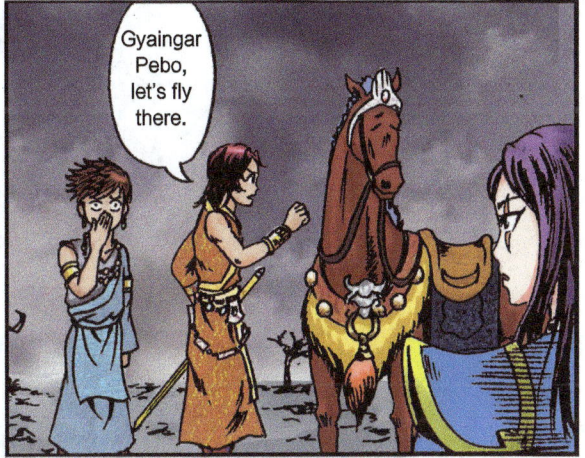

Gyaingar Pebo, let's fly there.

Shoo!

Gyaingar Pebo, you fall in love with this brainless fellow?

Shoo!

Gesar! We'd better kill her!

Wouldn't I lose face if I listened to you?

Whoa! That's enough!

Take that!

Pa!

Ping! Bang!

Pa!
Pa!
Pa!
Pa!

Holy light bomb!

038

040

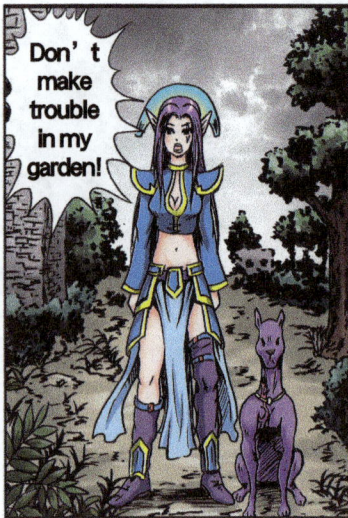

Don't make trouble in my garden!

Pa!

(Slurring) You seem to manage your life quite well.

He praised me.

You even understand what he said! Are you a Martian?

Why do you blush?

Gwa —

Cecho...

Chapter 3

Dream that Has Never Gone

Haha! It is wonderful here!

You really enjoy life. Is this garden your dowry?

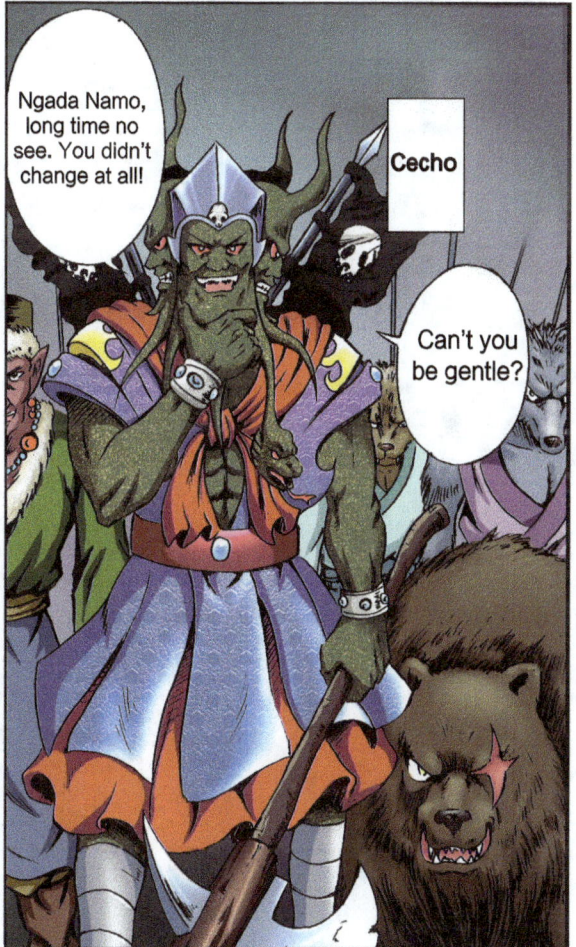

Ngada Namo, long time no see. You didn't change at all!

Cecho

Can't you be gentle?

Please go away. You are not welcome here!

I've come here for this.

The bear-headed monster has been beaten back into its original shape.

Have you seen a suspicious person?

I'm here alone. Go look somewhere else!

But...

？！

Do you know that man?

He is...

Cecho.

I will never forget what he did to our village.

But the devil is so powerful that no one in the state could defeat him.

Moreover, there are too many of them. We'd better...

Avoid confrontation with them.

Eek! Where is the guy?

Pa!

Hey, excuse me, are you Cecho?

Idiot!

This is...

Roar!

!

@#$@%&#!
(He's the man who has beaten me up!)

#!......!!(He is King Gesar of the State of Ling!）

@#

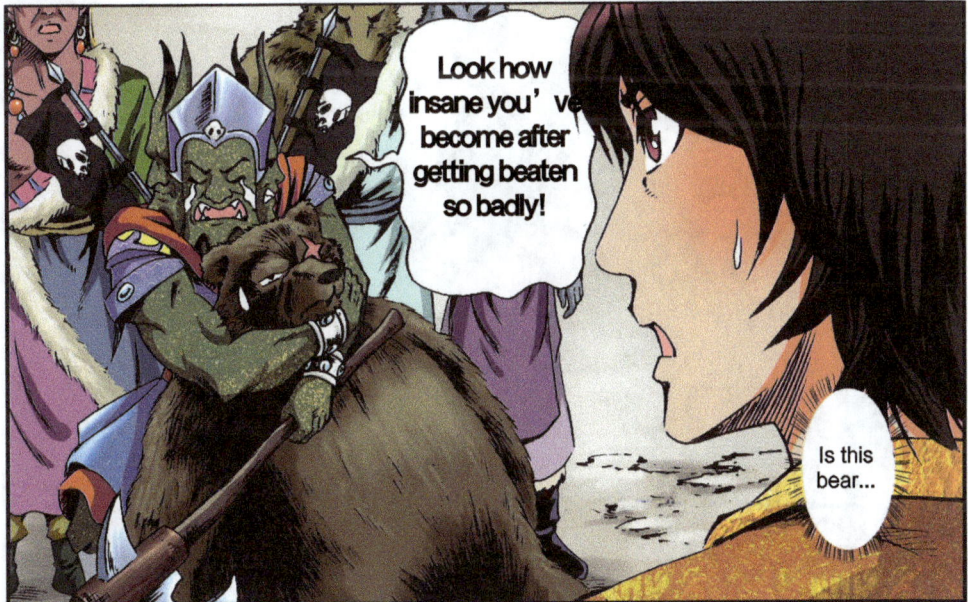

Look how insane you've become after getting beaten so badly!

Is this bear...

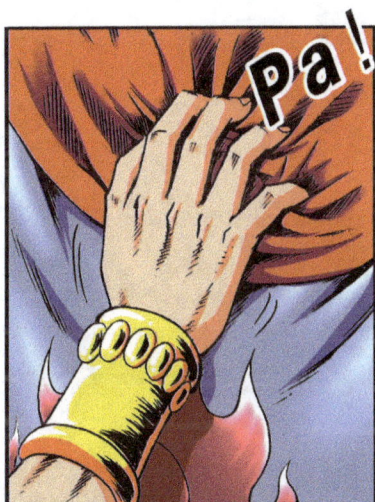

Cha!

Swish!

Whirr!

Whirr!

DBL
Holy light...

Pa!

Pa!

Whirr!

Sword!

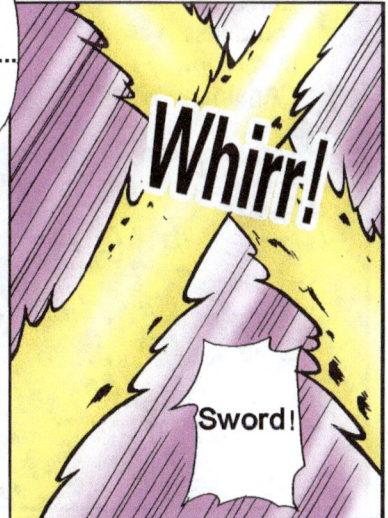

※DBL is the abbreviation of DOUBLE.

Haha... Little did I think you could last that long. Again!

It is so strange...

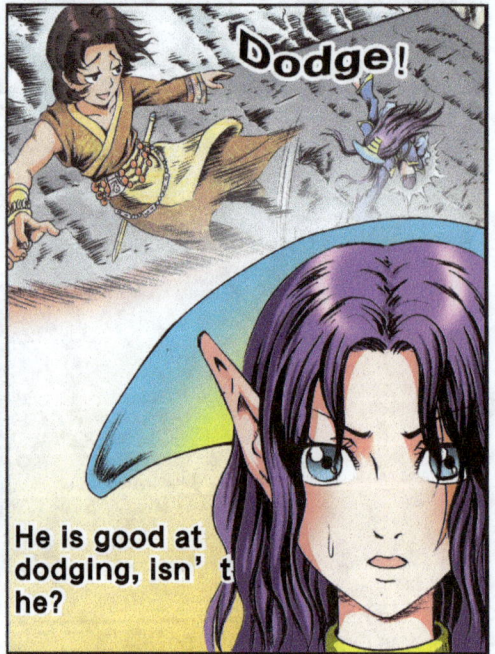

He is good at dodging, isn't he?

058

Whiz!

Whiz!

How dare you come here?

This is the Soul-Housing Sea.

So, fighting here,

We will be blessed by King Nortsam!

My fighting capacities will be doubled here.

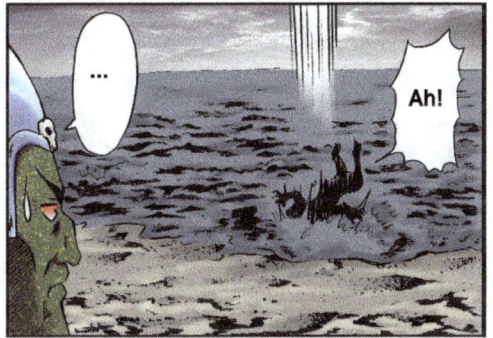

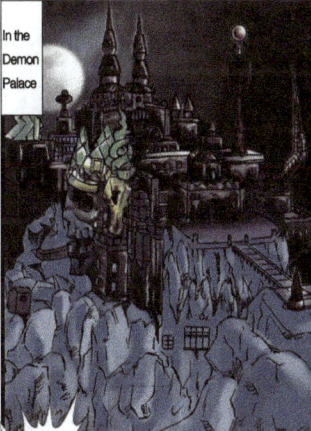

Queen?

She is the queen of the State of Ling...

Ngakar.

Since when were you interested in women?

Brother.

065

Chapter 4

Death Pasture

I can't! You do it!

Moreover, I don't know how to use this ring.

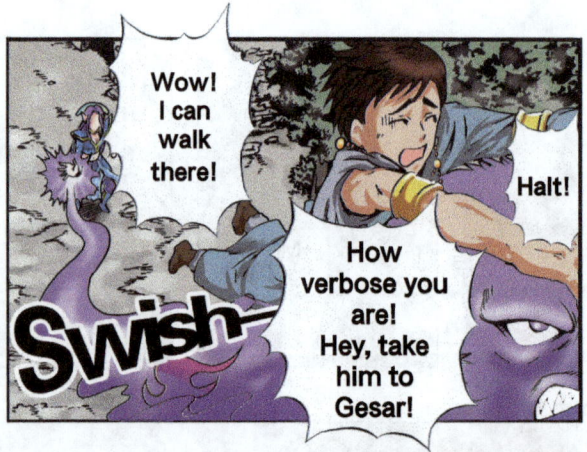

Wow! I can walk there!

Halt!

How verbose you are! Hey, take him to Gesar!

Swish—

Gesar. I'm coming to help you.

She asked me to tell you her name was Ngada Namo and...

Oh, I never thought she would help me...

Well, why do we go back?

Think!

Gyaingar Pebo~~

This guy hid in the garden.

Ta-ta

Do you see that? He is still eating!

Humph!

Gyaingar Pebo

Then... You enjoy yourselves here – I gotta go.

Cecho was finished. I will tell the good news to the surviving villagers.

Oh...

Bye!

I don't know why I feel like something's missing... Is that friendship? Do you see that?

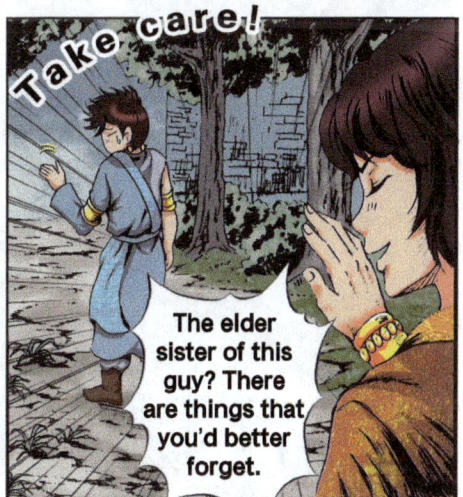

Take care!

The elder sister of this guy? There are things that you'd better forget.

We walked for another day after parting from Mofi...

All we saw is black and white!

Baa—

Chewin

A colorless world!

There is an old man over there.

Excuse me, but can I ask you something?

※Note: WWE refers to a popular wrestling match.

Don't look so smug!

Pa!

Hong!

Ping! Bang!

I see!

They've not become stronger, but we've got weaker?!

Hiss~

Ho ho, does it feel good to be deprived of strength?

Here is King Nortsam's...

Death pasture!

Since I got involved with that man...

Pa!

Pa!

Hey, hey! Didn't you agree to wrestle? The young people nowadays...

Well, no...

What about an archery contest?

What are the rules?

Shoot that yak.

Wait a minute! I need to clear my head.

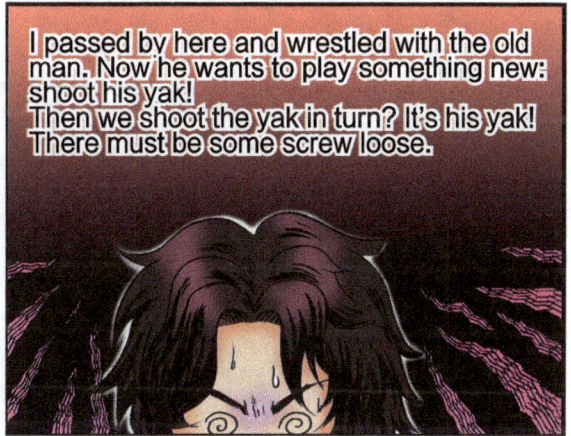

I passed by here and wrestled with the old man. Now he wants to play something new: shoot his yak!
Then we shoot the yak in turn? It's his yak! There must be some screw loose.

No time to lose. Come on!

I...

OK, let me have a try.

Pa!

Pa!

Holy light bow.

Holy light arrow.

Pa!

Pa!

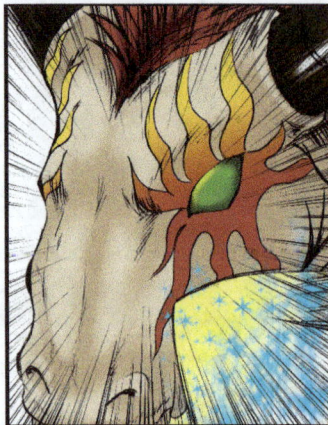

Chi—

How could the yak blow smoke?

Damn it! You missed the target!

It is not my fault... You...

You can't do anything! Go away if you don't want to die!

Whirr!

Hey, what is this? It spits...

Consecutive arrows of holy light!

Ao!

Double kill !

Pa!

Pa!

Whirr!

※Note: Double kill refers to the knocking down of two targets.

※Note: Hattrick is a football team. Here it refers to striking down three targets at one time.

084

Boy, good for you!

You killed the Soul-Housing Yak.

The magic has been removed once the yak died.

I have finally returned to myself.

I just hate to see it.

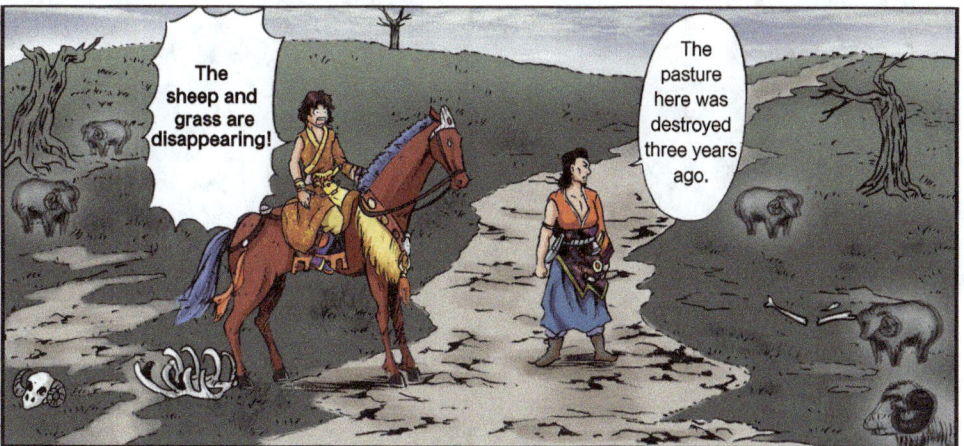

The sheep and grass are disappearing!

The pasture here was destroyed three years ago.

Chapter 5
Soul-Housing Tree

Were all these things done by Nortsam?

This goes too far.

Whirr—

If you want to see Nortsam, I will be your guide.

Well, who on earth are you?

I'm Chin'en, Minister of the Right under Nortsam.

Whirr!

Don't say this kind of thing casually.

You'd better explain to me what this is all about!

Pa!

Pa!

This guy gets mad so easily.

Don't misunderstand me!

I was controlled by Nortsam and could not help but obey.

He used the Soul-Housing Yak to imprison me.

Nortsam found I was to rebel.

It's my first time here. It is so exciting.

Chin'en, I feel Cholmo is very close to me.

Illusion?

It seems as if she was just standing behind me.

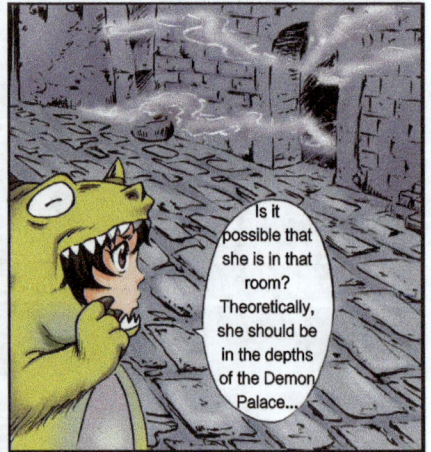

Is it possible that she is in that room? Theoretically, she should be in the depths of the Demon Palace...

Oh!

Are you...?

Call me Ngakar. Let me show you around.

Oh, Ngakar, I haven't got enough sleep recently.

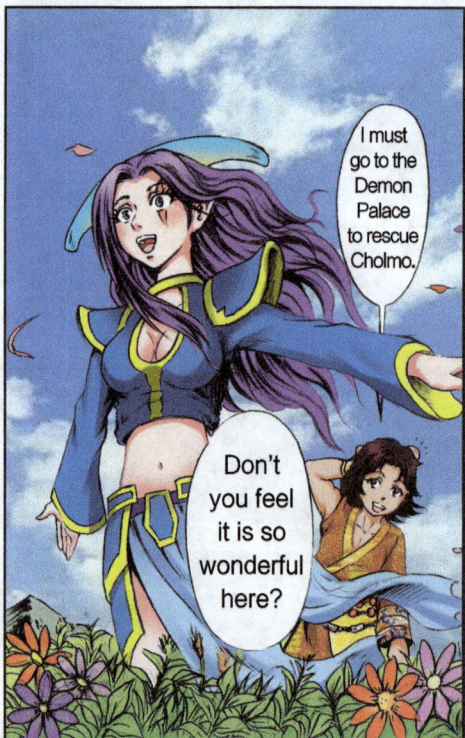

I must go to the Demon Palace to rescue Cholmo.

Don't you feel it is so wonderful here?

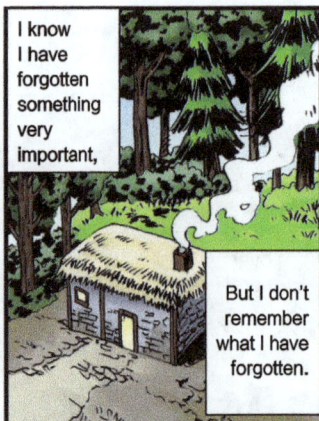

I know I have forgotten something very important,

But I don't remember what I have forgotten.

I just know I am very happy now...

Pa! Pa! Pa!

Perhaps I persued something; I lost something.

Rat=tat!

Rat-tat!

But they're not important now.

I think what I should do now is to...

Ta-ta-ta

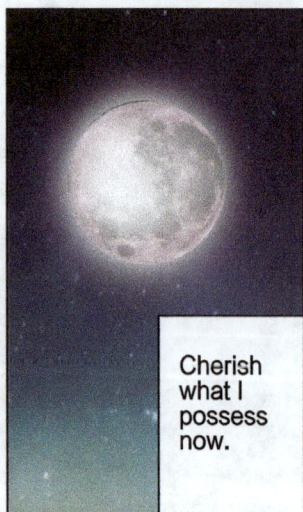

Cherish what I possess now.

Alas~~

What's the matter? What ails you?

No, but...

I just don't know how long we can live this way.

Don't woolgather.

I promise that I will be with you forever.

Cholmo.

King Nortsam.

It seems that the power of love is much stronger than your witchcraft.

104

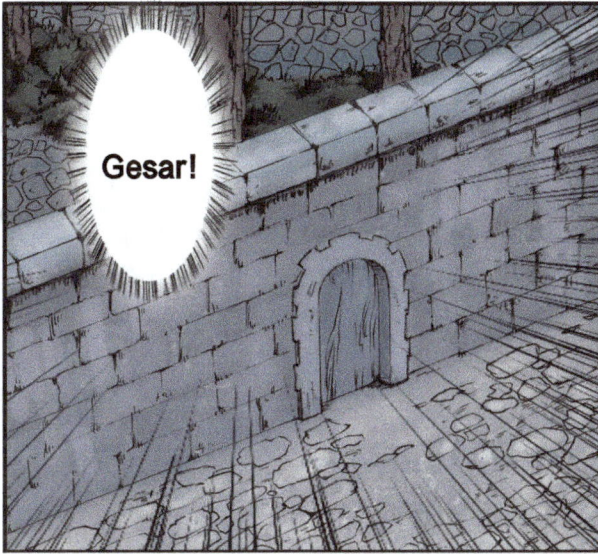

Gesar!

Perhaps I overrated you.

If this is all you can do...

Here will be your grave.

What's Next

Gesar's early encounters with adversaries test his burgeoning powers and resolve. As he prepares for greater challenges, the spiritual lessons he has learned become vital.

What new trials await him on his path to redemption? Proceed to Part 2 to explore Gesar's evolving role as a hero and warrior.*

www.ingramcontent.com/pod-product-compliance
Lightning Source LLC
LaVergne TN
LVHW022012080426
835513LV00009B/688